Greater Than Our Hearts

Greater Than Our Hearts

Ulrich Schaffer

HODDER & STOUGHTON
LONDON SYDNEY AUCKLAND TORONTO

Portions of this book were first published in German in the following books: *trotz meiner schuld*, © 1971 Oncken Verlag; *kreise schlagen*, copyright © 1973 by Oncken Verlag; *umkehrungen*, © 1975 Oncken Verlag; and *jesus, ich bin traurig froh*, © 1976 Ulrich Schaffer, published by R. Brockhaus.

British Library Cataloguing in Publication Data

Schaffer, Ulrich
  Greater than our hearts.
  1. Christian life
  I. Title
  248.4   BV4501.2

ISBN 0 340 33140 2

Hodder and Stoughton Editorial Office: 47 Bedford Square, London WC1B 3DP

This book is for all those who are looking for new ways of experiencing and living their faith in a rapidly changing world.

I wanted to share with you some of the thoughts and experiences of my growth. I have found it comforting to realize that other people are facing similar questions and trials. This book is my way of letting you know that you are not alone.

Contents

Like a Tree in the Earth

Sometimes It's Not
What It Seems

Confusions

What we consider to be need
  is often only the fear of becoming needy.
What we consider to be fear
  is often only the fear of being afraid.
What we consider to be pressure on us
  is often only the fear
  of being put under pressure.
When we are afraid because there is no way out
  it is often because we are afraid
  of not being able to see a solution
  and dreading that feeling.

We think we are free
  because others are even less free than we are.
We are happy
  because others look even less happy.
We think we are ready and prepared
  because we have thought of preparing ourselves.
We think we have given ourselves over to God
  because we intend to give ourselves.
We believe we are growing
  because we see others go backward.

Lord,
I am afraid
and live in the middle of fear.
But I know that this is only the beginning.
I know that I do not fully
affirm your testing of me
and that I am still living in illusions.

Show me where I am imagining things.
Show me where my feelings are sentimental,
   superficial and dishonest,
where I feel sorry for myself,
where I pretend to be in pain.
And teach me to experience
the joy in suffering,
the faith in danger,
and a yearning for your testing.

Hunger and Thirst

Without hunger and thirst
   you will not stand out among the well-fed.
Without hunger and thirst
   you don't have to look for fresh water.
Without hunger and thirst
   you will be satisfied with yourself.
Without hunger and thirst
   you will not understand the hunger and thirst of others.
Without hunger and thirst
   you don't need to cry.
Without hunger and thirst
   you will sleep well.
Without hunger and thirst
   you won't eat and grow anymore.
Without hunger and thirst
   you don't belong to the community
   of the hungry and thirsty.

Without hunger and thirst
you will not see God.
His mercy goes out to the yearning and searching.

The hunger and thirst in us
is the hand reaching out to God.

In hunger and thirst God is our teacher,
who creates in us the openness
to look for and to learn new things.

I Am Good to You

I am good to you
   and that is unfortunate
I have nothing against you
   and that is cowardly
I smile at you
   and it doesn't help you
I encourage you
   and that is bad
I am too patient with you
   and that allows you to regress
I close my eyes, not wanting to see
   and that allows you to remain blind
I say I love you
   and that is an expression of indifference
I mean well with you
   but that is not a challenge to you.

I am good to you
I have nothing against you
I smile at you
I encourage you
I am too patient with you
I close my eyes
I say I love you
I mean well

And all that shows
that I don't take you seriously
that I am playing with you.

I do not risk much
to break through to you.
I don't want to take chances
to lose the peace we have,
but really it's my fear of confrontation.

I leave
you behind
in your great loneliness.

Tell Me What You See

I live in my head,
in my thoughts,
which I reject or spin out,
which I like
or forbid to stay with me.

I know myself in these thoughts
and for me they construct the image
I have of myself.
There I live.
That is who I am.

Friend,
you don't know my thoughts
but you see my life.
You know what I do and what I neglect
and only through seeing me act
do you know what I think.

Tell me, therefore, what you see.
Do you see the Christ that I talk of,
does my life reflect what I say I believe?
Tell me what I live.
Tell me what you see,
I am so far away from my life.

Because We Have No Hope

When he enters the room
coldness enters with him.
We all know that.
We have experienced it often.

Today he came again
and each of us felt the cold
because we know him,
we have experienced it often.

It was like it always is:
he inhibited us and we became short,
the conversation became irritating.
But today he also suffered yet we didn't notice.

He had changed
and wanted to show us how different he was,
but we had no hope for him
and let him feel our coldness.

Telling Him What to Do

I keep on telling him what to do
because I love him.
I tell him what to change in his life,
what I would do in his position,
what to do differently,
what I see as the solution,
how to attack the recurring problem.
Because I love him.

Pray more!
Hold your ground!
Have you tried fasting?
Don't deny the Lord.
Accept and carry your cross!
Love.
Read the word more!
Argue less,
love more,
fight less,
yes, love more!
Look at those who are worse off.
Look at the Lord's suffering.
Be happy,
pray more!
I love you. I love you. I love you.

And then it suddenly strikes me:
my babbling,
my empty words,
not reaching my friend,
making him even lonelier,
more acutely aware of his predicament.

A shocking awareness begins to grow in me:
my friend is suffering
so that *I* will learn,
that I will finally see my inability to help him,
my lack of real love,
the emptiness of my attitude toward him,
my inadequate approach.
I see my unwillingness to suffer with him
unless I make his suffering
my own,
which takes more than words
and feelings of sympathy.

I am learning, Lord.
I am learning
in a painful way,
but I am learning.
Teach me.

Pressure

It is difficult to be shot down again and again
and then to bounce back again
just to be shot down again,
to come up just to be pushed under again.

And I ask you, Jesus,
whether that is really necessary.
Can't I live without it?
Can't I grow without it?
Can't I mature slowly?
Taking it easy,
learning from you,
but without all the hardships,
being confronted only with what I can handle?

Sometimes I feel that I can't grow
with all this pressure on me,
because to grow I need rest
and a time to collect myself.
I would like to control my growth
and the time of my growth.

That's what I would like,
but I sense that growth won't happen
under those conditions.
Therefore I will stay under your pressure,
I will affirm the difficulties
and standing in the face of them
I will grow strong.

Manufactured Faith

His faith is easy for him.
He seems to coast along without problems.
He does not see the paradoxes of life
or the inadequacy of his kind of faith.
He is content and takes everything in stride.

He tells me that he understands you, Lord,
but I do not sense his nearness to you.
His life does not convince me,
it seems empty and I wonder
where his contentment comes from.

I feel he has manufactured it
as he has manufactured his faith,
a faith that he learned about as a child
and to which he has clung up to this time.

Lord, he is afraid to let go
of this manufactured world,
of his manufactured God.
He is afraid to drop like a huge weight
into an abyss he cannot conceive,
because he does not really believe
that your hand is there to hold him.

Our faith in you only holds
because your faith in us is so great.

Christmas

You still walk the streets,
our streets,
looking for a place to put your head,
still poorer than a bird in its nest.

You still knock
on the double-latched bolted-shut door
with Christians inside.

Christ, you are still discarded
and dropped in the wastebasket
of sometime or never.

Christ
your chance is still slim
in our land of goodness and keep-smiling,
where we live by your ethics
without knowing you.
Proclaimed: teacher among teachers,
king among kings,
God among Gods,
one of the many ways to salvation,
take it or leave it.

Jesus, don't let me live outside of you,
outside of the heart of the world.
Smash down my locked door,
rest in my house
and sit at my table.
Let me be on your side,
drown me in your love.
Neglect the name and number that I am,
the address and place in or out of society
and break through to me
to release the weights
clinging to my hands and feet.

And love me into your love,
into your Christmas.

Short Biographies

If you are reading this, you are still engaged in writing your biography. You can still determine what it will be. You can still change.

1

Born,
died sixty years later.
In between: following and parroting of traditions
that he never understood
or digested.

2

In search of answers
without knowing where and what,
he found more
and meant more to many people
than he ever imagined.

3

The mystery of life
   movement
   which distinguished life from death
she did not have.

And it is true
what others say of her:
that she followed a dead God.

4

"To keep peace is the first order
of the Christian"
was the motto of his life.
He was faithful to it
right to his grave.

There was little difference
between his life and his grave.

5

His pious life
was the Christian disguise
for his flight from God.

Only his restlessness
insecurity and fear
gave him away
and showed what was really happening to him.

6

He drank milk all his life
for fear
of ruining his stomach with meat.

7

He was born when there were few Christians.
He died when there were few Christians.
But he lived his life
as a glowing example
of the changing power of Christ.

8

His life was led by others.
He had very little to do with it.

He sold his soul
for peace of mind and success
and his sale was successful.

His gravestone is more expensive
than those of fellow corpses.
But the earth into which he changes
is the same, all the same.

9

Sundays a Christian.
On other days as well.
When doing important things
and when following unimportant matters.

Undivided
when voting and praying,
when driving a car and when celebrating,
when writing letters,
when picking up the phone,
when reading, when eating,
when saying "hi" and when being silent,
when demonstrating and when resting.

A life
penetrated by the life of Jesus.

10

He did everyone justice.
Worked his way through all situations
without jarring anyone's sensibilities.

He had the capability
to know what was expected of him
and to do it almost before it was expected.

He could see all sides of a question:
racism, drugs, pornography,
capitalism, communism,
and for that reason he never became involved.
Consequently he was never wrong,
never lost an argument.
He was an expert on all questions,
loved and honored (in his carefully chosen circle
    of acquaintances),
conservative (progressive if it didn't cost anything),
liberal (but with a feeling for the past),
a free man but a Christian (according to his own
    interpretation).

He was a man who had made it.
What had he made?

Too Much

They have heard so much about you
in Sunday school,
cubs and guides,
young people's groups,
home builders.
And now they are in the middle of life
and can't hear,
can't see,
can't speak,
because they are overfed,
stuffed with your word,
made cheap by too much repetition.

What am I to say to them?

Lord, make me aware that you are listening
and weighing my words
and teach me to wait,
like you always waited for the right moment
in a person's life,
so that I won't contribute
to the hardening process
already so far advanced.

And above all
renew yourself in me.
Send me a hunger and a thirst
that will open me for a deeper life in you.

She Is So Together

She moves with elegance,
slightly aloof,
keeping that certain distance,
very aware of herself,
of her impression on others,
carefully choosing her words,
so conscious of her image
that she is unable to respond to others.

Yet actually she is tied in knots,
well-fashioned, good-looking knots,
but knots.

I am sometimes afraid of her
because of the dissecting look
with which she takes people and things apart
without really being interested
in putting them together again.

Yet in her togetherness I see her loneliness,
her dejection.
She is not happy with herself
but she has not yet come to the point
of admitting it, not even to herself.
She still has the feeling
that she must continue playing her role.

She has many people wondering
whether she really has a heart.

The Secret Loss

What do you gain
when you win an argument
  but lose the trust of people
when the others laugh at your jokes
  even when they are told
  at the expense of others
when you make more money
  but spend more
  so that your worries remain the same
when others say that you are "nice"
  because you avoid all confrontations
  but in the process lose your character
when you collect friends
  who seldom tell you the truth,
  who are hardly capable of telling the truth
  because they have no discernment
  and you have chosen them because of that
when you try to make an impression
  so that others will admire you
  but you still remain alone,
  perhaps more alone
  in spite of all their admiration
when you desperately try to look young
  but instead look like a caricature of yourself
  and never learn to become old

when you rush around to save time
   but you never learn to divide
   the time you have saved
   and end up having to kill it
   or to fill it up with a different rushing about
when you keep secrets about yourself
   so that others continue to believe
   in the image you have set up of yourself . . .

What do you gain?
Where are you going?
And then . . . ?

Jesus Meek and Mild

We want to fight against all images of you.
It is our manifesto
that you can be experienced in many different ways,
that you cannot be understood through dogma,
that you constantly change
in the way you appear to us.

Lord, our pictures are so unfair to you,
so one-dimensional
so oversimplified
without real life, without color.
We want to resist all pictures,
all confining theological images:
the gentle shepherd
the sweet Jesus
the baroque baby
the dear savior
the social reformer
the superstar.

You step out and leave each picture.
Each statue lies.
No dogma is sufficient.
Each truth about you runs the risk
of becoming untrue,
because you are the surprisingly different one,
who teaches us daily
to take you into our lives
in the new way in which you appear.

Success Stories

"Read the success stories of men who have found
power through faith."
—An advertisement for a series of books

Success stories
as in business
as in industry
as in academic life.

Success: the criterion
by which we measure ourselves
and others.

Making it (breaking others).
Sitting on top (looking down).
Comparing (being better).

How strange a success,
that of Christ dying on the cross.

Paradoxical

It's just impossible to get all the work done
because he is so busy
looking for more work.

He does not have time for anyone
because he is wrapped up in a project
designed to attract more people.

He has lost his ability
to meet a friend in love
because he just wants to convert that friend.

He keeps his eyes closed when praying
and asking for God's will
and therefore does not see
all the jobs to be done.

He is proud to be overworked.
He is proud of his restlessness,
of his super-organization,
of his poor health.

He does not have any free time
because he has to go to a committee meeting
to discuss free time and its application.

And so it goes on,
from one day to the next.
Life loses its coherence.
God's way of seeing things
disappears from our lives.
We spend our time
chasing and being chased.

Why do we then wonder
if God's love and blessing
do not show in our lives?

We Have Nothing Against . . . , As Long As . . .

We are not against pain and suffering
   because we know
   that they help us to grow and mature—
as long as it doesn't hurt too much.

We have nothing against a daily dying,
   we hear it from pulpits,
   read it in books,
   talk about it ourselves—
as long as we have the dying under control
and values remain stable.

We have nothing against a death in Christ,
   after all it's part of our doctrine—
as long as an apparent death is sufficient
for a resurrection.

We don't object to looking into the abyss
   because we know
   we owe that to those around us,
   particularly those who live without hope—
as long as we can still see the bottom of the abyss
and the reason for the void.

But when you take us at our word, Jesus,
when you get a hold of us
we quickly qualify our statements,
we limit what we say
and suddenly we are not quite as serious
   as we sounded.

We once again
choose the broad path
because on the narrow one
we feel too crowded,
too narrow-minded,
too serious.

When we are called to become a grain,
to fall to the ground,
to die,
then we would rather consider once more.

Jesus
make it clear to us
that there are no half-measures,
that we have to be totally immersed
into your dying
if we want to live with you.

In the Service of God?

A twenty-five-year-old man
who failed at many things in his life
because he did not want to make commitments,
because he had no sense of self-worth,
because he refused to be what he was,
because he wanted to be everything to everyone,
because he wanted more power than he could handle

has now decided to become a minister.
He is congratulated on his decision.
His parents are happy and so is his congregation.
Certain terms now elevate his pursuits:
full-time ministry, serving the Lord,
laying his life on the altar of God.

Actually there is very little spiritual
in his decision.
It is a power trip
that has finally found its expression
and a following in gullible parishioners,
who are still awed by a man who reads Greek
and gives his voice a special twist.

After three years at the seminary
he will emerge a different man.
In the eyes of the church he will be a pastor
and he himself will believe in his own rhetoric,
in his own stories.

Yet he has not changed.
I have just heard his sermon.

Marginal Notes

1

God sometimes becomes invisible
so that we can practice our eyes of faith better.

2

For God there are no "new" ways
of doing something
but only a dead or an alive heart.

3

God does not answer some prayers
because he has something better for us.

4

God was there before the Bible
and he will be there when all books are gone.

He is in the Bible
but also outside of it.

He speaks through the Bible
but also in other ways.

5

The investigating of our motives
must always be done by both:
ourselves and God.

6

When it is especially emphasized
that something is done in love
one has to be especially careful.

7

Both prophets and heretics
teach the unusual.

8

Noah was an egotist
when the time came to save himself.

9

The ability of Peter to walk on water
was directly connected
to the direction in which he was looking.

10

For God there are no "old" ways
of doing something
but only a dead or an alive heart.

In the Struggle of Living

One-thirty A.M.

In front of me
the emptiness of a sheet of paper
the loneliness of Elton John
80 on my radio dial
and the darkness of this hour.

In six hours it will be light
and around me an expectant world
will be waiting for a breakthrough
in a thousand different areas of life.

They will be waiting for You
without even knowing it.

How weak I feel.

Eighteen and Lonely

How difficult it must be
to be eighteen and lonely.
Not to belong to the crowd
that runs around together,
does things and enjoys life.

She is lonely because she thinks.
She is aware of her vulnerability.
She is a compulsive thinker,
can't stop her wheels from turning.
She has to analyze,
check out,
reject or accept.

She is in constant change,
always becoming
because she wants to live every second,
wants to be truly alive
without following a deadly pattern
devoid of all life.

But she does not want this life.
She wants to be rid of all this depth.
She wants to be like all the others,
just carrying on,
not digging too deep,
but she finds she can't be like that anymore.

Lord, I know that we are fearfully made,
that nothing is coincidence,
none of our thoughts and actions.

You have allowed the many thoughts
to enter her head,
to cause confusion or to enlighten her
in your loving search for her.
I know you will get through to her.
You will transform her life
even if you don't take the weight of living from her
You will teach her all about perspective,
about seeing things your way
and about the riches to be found in suffering.

Until then Lord, help me
to be understanding,
encouraging her to hang on,
not to give up,
not to return to a life
which is not really hers.
And let me learn from her life.

He Is Missing Today

He is missing today,
walking right by it,
thinking of everything but today.
His thoughts are in the unchangeable past or
in the future.
He dreams of things that never were
and probably never will be.

He needs to be liberated
to live in the present,
to experience the beautiful vibrations of life
as they pour into his senses
and light up in many colors,
as they rush past not to be held,
not to be called back,
not to be anticipated,
but just to be taken as they come.

Help him, Lord,
to affirm the unique present,
to live the holiness of each moment,
to be filled with your presence.

At This Moment

Now
thousands are dying in the world.
Now
someone is being shot.
Now
someone is being robbed.
Now
someone is being raped.

While I am writing this
while you are reading this.

Now
someone is pronounced guilty.
Now
someone is losing all hope.
Now
someone is yearning for the end.
Now
someone is cruelly tortured.
Now
someone is deciding for evil.

In London, Hamburg, Leningrad, Sydney,
San Francisco, Vancouver, Calcutta and Buenos Aires,
in the villages and cities of the world.

But now He is also walking through the world.
Now He is beaten, shot, robbed and tortured.
Now He is dying for us,
to lift the curse and make us free.

47

Losers

He tried so hard.
He fought like a lion.
He cried much.
He was so lonely
but he fought on.
He tried over and over again
but nothing came of it.
He was a loser
and he knew it.
That is why he fought so hard.

All the fighting
brought great losses
and all the losses
brought greater losses.

Now he has stopped fighting.
He rests in the earth.
Grayness covers him.

Behind him he leaves a family still fighting
against even greater odds,
not getting anywhere.

One by one they are giving up,
dying slowly,
bit by bit,
day by day,
loss by loss,

defeat by defeat,
death after death
until finally that last death
will give them peace.

That is hard to take, Lord,
for them
and even for us,
who are looking on
so helplessly.
It leaves us wondering
how all of this fits together.

Life Speaks Louder

Lord, be merciful,
shut me up
when my life
speaks so much louder
than my words.

When we blunder through life,
golden-throated and silver-spooned,
bungling it all,
be merciful, Lord,
shut us up.

Let us feel our own lies.

New Direction

How often do I have to stop
and
turn around
because I can't go on
with my empty actions.

When turning I notice
fear and happiness.

Because turning around means:
to turn away from my dreams
to discern the illusions among my ideas
to become free.

Turning around means:
to meet again
that which I left behind me long ago,
which I thought I had mastered.

Turning around means:
to suddenly meet new people,
to be confronted by unusual situations,
to give up false obligations.

Turning around means:
to see the tracks of my own life,
to change direction,
to take a path that will lead on.

Dark Shadow

Today a dark shadow followed me
and I could not shake it off.
Yet there was no reason
for all this darkness.

And you, Lord,
let me remain in this darkness all day,
you thought it right
to let me suffer through this.

Now it is past midnight,
the pressure is slowly lifting,
I am being liberated
and I can feel your presence again.

I am on your level again,
but suddenly it dawns on me
that I was on your level all the time
without noticing it.
And I realize
how important it was to go through that.

How else would I learn to share your suffering?
How else could my life ever have the weightiness
that your life had?
I would only increase your suffering
with my superficiality.

Now I can praise you as the shadow
   and as the liberator,
as the one who strikes us
   but also as the healer,
as the stranger who pushes us away
   but at the same time
   as the friend reaching out to us.
I praise you as the one who takes us
   to depths of insight we have not reached before
and as the one who wants to share his darkness
   his suffering and pain
   with us,
   if we are willing.

Her Insecurity

She is turning people off
and she doesn't even understand why.
She won't listen to anyone,
won't believe when people tell her
what she has to change in her life.

She gets so desperate.
She fights as though someone
were trying to take her life.
She defends herself
with all the weapons at her command:
she becomes snippy,
she laughs condescendingly,
she becomes bitter,
with irony in her voice she snaps at people.
And finally she tears apart and destroys.

I know, Lord,
it's her way of living with her insecurity,
of not giving in to anyone,
not even you.
It's her way of prolonging the agony.

Teach me to stand firm in this flood of despair,
not to give up,
not to be turned off,
not to deny her these emotions,
but to be like you,
a positive vibration,
a pillar of love,
dedicated to stand when others run away.

A Chance

He doesn't stand a chance,
you know it.
He is really washed up.
They have pushed him aside
in their struggle for the top.
He was kind
and didn't push anyone around to move up.
But now he has had enough.
He is using their techniques,
their tactics,
their hate and falseness.
He is biting and spitting
and spilling his disgust over everything.
And yet he doesn't have a chance
because he can't really play their game.

Hold him, Lord,
before he goes under,
before he reaches the point of no return.
Hold him
and give him a healthy distance to it all.
Hold him
because I can't do it.
He doesn't trust anyone anymore.

With your help
he still has a chance.

He Is Knocking Himself Out

He is knocking himself out,
trying to be with it,
trying to be in everything,
trying to please everyone,
trying to be a picture-book Christian.

His clothes demonstrate this.
He has the laugh of a man
who associates with the right people.
He can be both young and old,
far-out and straight,
depending on what is required.

He turns on to the right things,
he swings,
he knows where it's at,
he's got it all together.

Jesus, I wonder just who he is
because he is living his life
according to images put on him.
He is living secondhand.
He is living several lives,
of which not one is his own.

He is afraid of becoming himself,
feeling that without trappings
he will be too uninteresting,
not spectacular enough.

Lord, help him to see
that people can't really communicate with images,
with unreal people,
with super-real people.
Help him to see
that everyone is only looking for someone
who will share himself and be open,
someone with weaknesses,
someone who is not always in control of life,
not some understudy
of a second-rate movie actor.

Show him the beauty of himself
in his buried self
and help him to dig it up.

Speaking Your Word

Lord, I spoke your word today
and it brought about confrontation,
it brought hardship and resentment
and I did not want it
but it has happened.

Now I am blaming myself
and would like to undo what I have done.
I can't stand the tension,
I want to set things right
(even though I know they are right now).
I want to excuse myself,
want to make up,
but I know I shouldn't.

How can I take back your word?
I would only snuff out
the flame of growing awareness
because I know you were talking to him,
speaking your word
through me.

Again and again
I expect life to be easy on me,
but how can I expect more than you had?
You were not loved
when you spoke openly.
You were despised
but you never took back
what your father had told you to say.

You lasted through that tension.
You stuck it out.
You were silent when least expected
and very vocal
when it was not wanted.

You did not live by good manners
or according to the expectations
of the world around you.
You did not fill your time with small talk,
hiding the truth.

You lived for your father
and were loved for it
and scorned for it.
How can we ask for more?

No Shortcut

He was told to praise the Lord,
he was subtly pressured to praise
and now he praises.
But his inhibitions won't leave him,
he can't get off the ground,
there is no liberation
and he is surprised
because he was promised so much.

Lord, help him to accept
that there is no shortcut to liberation
that we can't make our own liberation
and show him the goodness
and the honesty
of a heavy heart
before you.

I Want to Come to You

I want to come to you,
that is why I am showing you
who I am.

Show me who you are
because we are very similar
and we will recognize each other.

We have to stand in the light,
not hide,
if we want to become one.

She Is Becoming Older

Each day she is becoming older
by more than a day
because she is waiting so much
for him.

As a child
she had already pictured the happiness of marriage
and as a teenage girl she had taken great care
to make herself beautiful,
waiting and waiting.

Then came her first fear of "being left over."
Her parents just laughed
because they could not understand her fear,
and she was all tied in knots.

Then he came
but did not understand her either.
He did not know how to call forth
her inner beauty
and left her sadder than before.

Her friends married,
had children and raised them,
while she became more lonely
from year to year.
That is her sad and heavy life.

Jesus, reach down into her loneliness
and show her other ways of being fulfilled,
that her life can be full to the brim
with joy,
whether she marries or not.

Help her to affirm your choice for her,
help her to stop blaming herself
and to see the richness found beyond roles.
Help her to find her uniqueness.

Thank you
that there are many ways of loving
open to us
and that each way is complete.

A Secret

She has not fixed her past.
She is dragging it around with her
and her love for him is not getting off the ground.
Although she is pretending
that everything is all right
she can't even convince herself.

And he wonders what is still separating them.
She is not open but elusive.
He feels that he is holding a secret in his hands
when he is holding her.

He is right.
She has a secret with another man.
Not that she is leading a double life,
no, not at all, it happened long ago.
And yet she has never set it right.
She believed that time would take care of it
but now she begins to see
that this secret binds her.

Lord, give the strength to set things right
and a real love for openness
so that their relationship
can bloom and grow.

Hitchhiker

I picked him up as he was thumbing.
His longish hair suited him.
The guitar seemed real,
not just a put-on.
He seemed relaxed,
but there was much sadness about him.

His life seemed drowned in meaninglessness,
held together only by the habit of living,
by daily duties,
and motions that count off minutes,
hours and days.

Looking at him
I saw his life change before my eyes.
I saw his talents develop,
saw his life receive direction,
saw his questioning take on different forms.
I saw him smile and grow
as I imagined Christ in his life.
Then he had to get out.

Don't let him get too far,
catch up to him.

Biography

Born twenty years ago
into a marriage that was never a marriage
and still has not become one,
but is rather a convenient form of prostitution.

He went through the mill of trying to belong at 14,
of going steady at 15 because of peer pressure,
of temporarily dropping out at 16,
of giving up school at 17,
and of taking on odd jobs (which he did not like)
to support his lifestyle.

At 18 he was on the way to becoming a father,
which he stopped,
leaving him full of guilt, which he hid.
He was forced to become tough,
which he expressed by changing his language.
At 19 a real bitterness set in,
which left him a cripple for human relationships.
Now he does not trust anyone.
He cannot afford feelings.
He will not accept help.

He is spaced out,
very untogether, shy, scared,
and he points an accusing finger
in every direction.

He seems to have stepped out of a psychology text:
a classical case,
a type,
an example of alienated youth,
typical of a whole segment of the young generation
and therefore we don't have to deal with him
individually.
We can just say: yes,
that's what they're like!
Isn't it a pity,
I feel so sorry for them all.

And we don't realize
that we are also behaving like "types,"
examples of the other side of the coin,
hiding in our collective indifference.

Jesus,
teach us to meet each person individually,
to become concerned with the suffering
of one specific person
in specific time and space.
Help us not to lump together
in impersonal groups
the very personal suffering
of real people.
Help us to believe in your changing power.

Breaking Through

We talked and did much
to avoid the real issues
because we did not want to risk talking about
what really concerns us
and not one of us dared to stop the charade.

Now we have gone our separate ways again
more lonely than before
and yet the deep wish for a "you,"
the wish to become transparent,
to see and to be seen,
remains as a yearning in us.

Lord help us
to break through the decorum and order of society
that is really a disorder
because it makes us into strangers
to each other
as we continue talking about
the weather, cars, food prices.

Help us to break through to what counts.
Help us to find one another.

Public Confession

I have various friends and acquaintances
who expect me to see the world in their way.
They would like to convert me
to what they believe,
perhaps to create a greater harmony and security.
I have to watch
that I don't do the same to them
without noticing it.

I have acquaintances who love Jesus Christ,
but they talk and live in a way
that makes their faith unbelievable to others.
Nothing about it seems attractive
and consequently no one wants to live like that.

I have acquaintances
whose theology seems impeccable,
but in search of the right theology
they have forgotten how to live.
All they have is a lifeless faith.

I have friends
who have answers to all questions,
but whose answers
leave the questioners unsatisfied.

Further, I know people
who have no answers
and they have made a science of this.
They stamp as superficial everyone
who dares to have an answer.

Then there are those
who are pious and churchy,
or not pious and not churchy,
or those who do not believe in anything
but still would like to be called Christians.
There are those who are first and foremost
Baptists, Presbyterians, Catholics,
Lutherans, Methodists,
and they see their answer in this membership.

These friends and acquaintances
categorize me in short order
by comparing my faith with theirs.
I receive the following titles:
—one who fell by the wayside
—a standard Christian
—a freethinker
—someone you can't figure out
—someone who is pious but not pious enough
—someone who is a Christian
    but not church-oriented enough
—a searcher who is searching in the wrong places.

Or sometimes these friends do something
that is even harder for me to deal with:
they adopt me and count me as one of their own,
in the shortsightedness that we all share
when we follow a certain path with blinders on.
When this happens
I have to defend myself.

When looking at my friends
I come to the conclusion
that I don't want to live up to the expectations
of anyone anymore.
I will not survive this life if I do.

I will not make myself fit
for anyone anymore.
I will not do "what a Christian does"
and I will not refrain from doing
"what a Christian refrains from doing."
I will do what I consider to be important,
I will do what I realize and can back
with my whole character.
Otherwise I would be lying.

I cannot be more pious
    because he wants it.
I cannot talk differently about Jesus
    than I am doing
    without being fake.
I cannot be more "into" the church
    because she wants me to be.
I cannot say "Amen"
    when I feel like screaming.
I will not scream
    when I want to say "Amen."
I cannot smile
    when I feel like crying.

I will not split up my life
   the way you want me to
   into spiritual and worldly
   into faith and life
because I am only *one* person
   with *one* past
   with *one* heart
   and *one* face.

When I do that my friends suddenly step back
because I become uncomfortable for them.
The wolf in sheep's clothing becomes apparent.
I am dangerous
and they push me away
in a friendly but definite manner.

Now I am looking for people
who dare to be what they are,
who have only *one* face,
who do not want to be liked at all costs
and therefore are often not liked
by the beautiful people.
I am looking for people
who do not do what is "Christian,"
separating their life and faith.
I am looking for people
who do not seek shelter
in the name of a group
or in some membership.
I am looking for people
who can stand alone before God
and bear it.

Like a Tree in the Earth

My Faith in You

My faith in you
is like clay on the wheel of the potter,
formed and fired.

In constant change it is molded
to create me in your image,
a likeness of praise.

My will is fixed on you
and when it wavers
I lose the ground under my feet.

I am joined to you by my sin
and by your death,
bound together in the tumble through life.

Lord, I am anchored in you
like a tree in the earth,
held between life and death,
in the ground of faith
which you are.

Everywhere

Without boundaries
your praise travels across the earth
for those who know you.

The sun
becomes a mirror of your love for me,
my great God.

You are gentle
like the grasses in the evening breeze.
You love me in spite of my guilt.

In the snow
I see your purity
which makes me pure.

You are a circle
without beginning and end
compassionately surrounding me.

I can see you,
yet I am only a human being
amazed that I can know you.

Kingdom of God

The kingdom of God
is inside you.
>   —Jesus

God's kingdom is where the king is
and he is in you and in me
—not tied to buildings of wood or stone
—not tied to names or titles
—not tied to times and plans
—not tied to language and expressions
—not tied to our abilities and inabilities
tied only to the possibility
of living in you and me
as lord of life.

Are we in the kingdom
and is the kingdom in us?
Or are we tied to a visible kingdom?
Even if we talk of the kingdom
but don't carry it in us
we will be talking into the wind.

It is never more important
to *do* something for God
than it is to *be* in God.

Reversals

Lord, I love you
because you are so different,
you are so deep
that I can never understand you completely
and that is why my life with you
is exciting.

A new world opens up to me,
   your world,
the same world as before
but now seen through your eyes,
a world in which the first become the last
and the despised
become the chosen,
a world in which the poor
are immeasurably rich,
and wisdom is measured
by closeness to you.
A world full of changes,
life full of reversals
and new perceptions.

At your side
I want to discover
the world around and in me,
to move from surprise to surprise,
to become rich
by living with you.

Learning to Lose

I learn to lose:
my valuable free time
my peace and order
my good conscience
my security

but more:
my gifts
my successes
my memories of things spiritual
my high goals
the joy of repentance

yet more:
your nearness
your consolation
your word
your plans with me
your expected leading

but still more:
even you, Lord, I have to lose,
you have to slip out of my secure grip
so that I will have to regain you differently
than I have ever had you.

Nothing Is Coincidence

I don't believe in coincidence anymore
because I know
that that which seems coincidental
is exactly the plan
God is pursuing for my life
with loving certainty.

Above all coincidences
I see the palms of hands
into which is written my name:
Ulrich Schaffer
you belong to me,
stay with me,
I love you.

I Strain Toward You

I want to express
what is in me
so much.

I strain toward You,
overcome by the wish
to be with You,
to stand illumined by You,
transformed in Your insight.

But I cannot express
who I am
and what my deepest yearning is.
Everything I say
is said with inadequate words
and on a level that does not do justice
to what I feel.

And so I stand before You,
tired out once again
by all the attempts
to stand in Your center
and to break through my limitations.

I hope You will hear
more than my words.

I Can't Go On

Lord,
I can't go on,
meaning has left everything
and I don't know
what I can do.

Here, Lord,
I will just drop
into the abyss,
into the fullness of your hand.

Here, Lord,
I will stand empty.
I am waiting to be rescued
but can't wait much longer.

Here, Lord,
I am drowning,
but I will believe
that it is in the fullness of your love.

Greater Than Our Hearts

You might not remember
  but He died for you.
You might not believe it
  but He cares.
You might not consider yourself important
  but He does.
You might not accept it
  but He has forgiven you.
You might not sense Him
  but He is with you.
You might condemn yourself
  but He has chosen to love you.

He sees us differently,
He is so much more,
so much greater than our hearts.

Jesus I Love You

I love you more than ever
and more than I can say.

I love you when I let my fingers
    run along the bark of a birch
    feeling the strength and life.
And when in the mornings
    I pull back my curtains
    and see the fog on the ocean.
When I see a bee
    disappearing into the calyx of a flower.
I love you when the setting sun dips me in blood
and when the fir snaps in the fierce storm.
I love you when the pebble skips on the water
    and doesn't want to sink.

I love you for all the failures in my life
    which drove me into your arms,
for the loss of my mind
    in order to win your wisdom.
I praise you for all that was incomprehensible
    which caused me fear
    and showed me the vulnerability of my life.
I praise you for all the surprises
    which have shaken me up
    and opened a new world for me.

I thank you for your nearness
    which fills my life with joy
    even when I feel alone and at the mercy of fear.
Thank you Jesus—my friend.

Sounds of Life

I catch the sounds of life
as they penetrate and spread out in me.
The sound of neighbors in their garden.
A dog barking on the street below.
A child playing nearby.
My wife talking to her niece,
digging deep into the problems of life.

These riches strike me
in precious seconds,
manifesting Your abundance,
Your wealth showered on me
now.

Stimulation to the overload.

We

Lord,
we are
bent and beaten
weighed down and ground to dust,
dispersed and scattered,
no more than wind,
yet we are loved ones.

God,
don't withdraw your heaviness.
Bent we are close to you
and you are
ground and earth beneath us.
And every bending
and every breaking
bends and breaks us
toward you.

In Everything

Jesus,
again and again I meet you
   when talking to people who love you
but also in people
   who don't know you.

You surprise me
in John Lennon singing "Imagine,"
in the play by Arthur Miller,
in the short notice in the newspaper,
in the talk by Germaine Greer
   about the freedom of women,
in the films of Ingmar Bergman,
in the documentary on TV,
in the paintings of Andrew Wyeth,
and in the confusion of international politics.

Suddenly you are here,
in my living room
with prophets and teachers
   who don't even realize it themselves
and you speak to me.

I notice that you are not tied
   to the willingness of your children
   to be used by you,
that everything can be used by you
if you want to talk to this world.

Lord make me able
to see your hand in my life
in everything.

Your Peace

Lord, I notice how close you come to me.
You step up to me
with your peace,
you show me
what is really important.

I relax
and forget all the unimportant details
which always loom too large in my life
in your absence.

The experience of this hour
in the midst of all that is so transitory
is precious beyond words.

You are close to me
in my feelings,
in my mind,
in my spirit.
You are everywhere with your gentleness.
You are hesitant
because you respect our freedom
and won't force yourself on us.

You are more than words,
more than any possible expression:
your closeness
your hands
your eyes which guide us.

As Darkness Sets In

Looking at you
I overcome
and am overcome
by your light
dispelling all darkness.

I am broken
and yet I fly.
I deny all heights and depths
and break through into your kingdom of light.
I am held by you
in the certainty of loving you
and wanting to love you
whatever may be happening around me.

I have decided to experience
the richness of life
in spite of the many difficulties
and even when I become weak
and can't see any more,
when I stagger and reel,
I will cling to my faith
and my experiences with you
will carry me through.

Keep me, Lord,
darkness is setting in.

Before Me and in Me

The battle is not over
but the tenseness is gone.
I sense victory.

I lean against your shoulder
my God
and rest.

I notice how your ears hear
   even when I whisper.
I notice how you hurry
   to assure that I will be well.
How you are wakeful
   to give my life direction.

And in me everything calls out to you
my beautiful Lord:
the endlessness of your works
the warmth of your eyes
the eyes looking at me in love
the certainty with which you guide your hand.

I will walk in your light,
break through walls and shackles,
cloaked in your security,
saved from the emptiness
which is opening up
in me and before me.

You Are Sufficient

Jesus I come to rest
in the knowledge
that you are all I need.

When I am sad
I place my sadness on you
and I am comforted.

When I am happy
I throw my joy toward you
and you double it.

When I am searching
I come to you
and find.

When I am bound
I hold my chains out to you
and you release me even if my chains remain.

You are sufficient
because you completely surround me.
I need nothing else.

I Am Losing My Sorrow

I am losing my sorrow
which is so light, so superficial,
tied to some words
that might not even have been meant
the way I heard them.

But there remains a scar from each hurt,
making my life richer,
teaching me maturity
in the face of my dejection.

The knowledge of vulnerability
is constantly with me.
I am aware of the smallness of my life
about to be over at any time,
like a leaf of grass
or the song of a bird.

Here and Now

Here and now, Lord,
it matters what you mean to me.
My past experiences were great,
but I need you here and now
because each day is a new start,
full of trials and obstacles.

I don't want to pressure you,
don't want you to act prematurely.
I don't want to see miracles,
all I ask for is a solid faith,
your most beautiful gift,
here and now,
so I can make it through the time
that you are invisible.

Only You

My wish is
to come only to You,
to put aside and reject everything else
to stand before You
and to wait.

Not to waste my time anymore
with words and actions
that don't count before You
and make me dishonest.

To order my life in a new way,
to consider what forms me,
and how others are formed through me
and then to reject or emphasize more.

Let it become visible in my life
that You are the pearl
for which I will give up everything.

That in You is my treasure
and my heart.

Jesus, I Am Happy Sad

We all carry on some sort of dialogue with ourselves, with others, with God, without actually talking. We are moved by something. We take a stand. Generally we see only one side at first—our side—the most obvious side. Then we go on thinking and realize that there are other ways of seeing. That is a form of dialogue, of talking to ourselves. We become a partner to ourselves and are enriched by the different views we take of an issue: I see it this way . . . but then it can also be seen that way . . . and taking that into account. . . . If we do this talking to ourselves in a creative way, and do not only try to defend our first impressions or opinions, then we will learn to hear what God has to say to us. Then we become engaged in a dialogue with God.

Perhaps this section can help you to take more seriously the various voices you encounter in yourself. We have to learn not to deny the voices in us that seem at first to be contradictory to what we have thought until now. How could we ever grow? A dialogue with ourselves is a good way to begin a meaningful dialogue with God.

The meditations of this section attempt to focus on the kind of dialogue we may have with ourselves. The first meditation in each group states the first way of seeing a subject, the initial reaction. Then other voices follow. Some may continue the first voice, others may take the opposite view, some may question what has been said, others may try to delve into the motives of a particular point of view.

There is movement from statement to counter-statement, from accusation to self-accusation, to insight, to conviction. Every new way of seeing casts light on the original concern. Some answers give rise to new questions, some questions become answers when formulated more clearly. Some meditations remain totally open. Others seem rounded off like final answers, but these must also be checked out and questioned again. The emphasis in this section is on "process." Faith is dynamic, moving, becoming.

You might try to read only the first meditation in a given set, then close the book and see what sort of dialogue develops. Perhaps this developing dialogue could then be written down as a personal continuation of this section of the book.

Multiple Vision

Jesus
I am thrown this way and that,
opinions come and go,
everything seems possible,
everything seems impossible.

My way of acting
must be right,
on the other hand
it can't be right.

My words were spoken too harshly,
but on the other hand
they were not clear enough
or perhaps they were said at the wrong time.

I don't want to participate in a certain action,
but on the other hand it is important for me
   not to withdraw
   because then I will not learn
   nor will I be a corrective to the others.

I want to,
but I don't want to,
yet I know I should want to,
but I also know
that I do not want to
because I think I should want to.

I am standing between alternatives.
I am happy sad.
I am a person faced with decisions,
having to give answers,
having to take a stand on issues.

Jesus, take away my fear
of all the different voices that I hear daily,
in order to learn to hear
what you want to say to me
in every voice.

Overwhelmed by Joy

1
I experienced it again today.
You were suddenly there
with your surprising presence.

You were suddenly there
without any visible reason,
without my having done anything,
without preparation,
without warning.
Suddenly you were there
with your complete joy,
with the relaxation which emanates from you,
with the sense you put back into life.

There you are
and I can only smile
at how connected everything is in my life.

I sense your liberation
and I see that you have come to me
as a human being again
and I am happy to live in that realization.

2

I become strong in this joy.
My life receives a new elasticity
and becomes interesting for others.

but only because this joy
   is in contact with you
because all manufactured, drummed-up joy
   leaves a great emptiness behind.

3

But I also know
that this joy
which seems so secure now
can come to an end very quickly.

I don't want to think about that.

4

Yes,
I do want to think about that
because the beginning of joy,
the climax of joy,
and the end of joy
all come from God,

for those who love God.

5
Then the amazing thing happens:
joy becomes a background
on which my entire life takes place,
a security which allows me
to bear all uncertainty.

A background that is hardly noticeable
yet creates solidity and perspective
in the picture.

Alone with Jesus

1
When I am sad
they want to cheer me up
by saying:
—it'll get better
—don't let it affect you so much
—we understand what you are going through.

And by doing that
they achieve the opposite
because I am not looking for pity
and well-meant suggestions.

Again and again I notice
that they want to cheer me up
so that their life with me will be easier,
that I won't get on their nerves as much,
that I won't make them ill at ease
by seeing things differently.

But no one really wants to join me.
No one wants to go through what I am going through
and no one is really interested in my thoughts.

Are you still with me Jesus?

2

Perhaps I am to learn
that if I share my thoughts with another person,
this sharing will already change those thoughts.

Perhaps the moment has come
for me to enter my thoughts much more deeply
    than before,
to penetrate them
and to find their hidden motives.

3

I notice
that I want to share with others
much too quickly
and that my feelings and thoughts
remain superficial because of it
because talking often simplifies things
beyond the point to which they should be simplified.

4

Jesus stands across from me
He lets me think my thoughts to the end.
He does not interrupt me.
He does not even stop
    that which might go in the wrong direction.
He does not hold me back
    from entering something more dangerous,
but rather he gives me the freedom
    in which I become independent.

Just Before Giving Up

1
I was among people again today
who are light-years away from me,
whose jokes depress me,
whose superficiality irritates me,
whose insensitivity makes me feel insensitive.

Now at the end of the day
I feel dirty
and everything tender and subtle
seems to have left my life.
I am about to give up
trying to make deeper contacts.

My life seems to consist only of tiredness.

2
But then I have to think of him
who spent 33 years among those lost and blind,
who saw their dullness,
who experienced their insensitivity
    and brutality
and yet he did not give up the world
but continued to participate in it
and spent much time with individuals
who found a new life through him.

And often he remained lonely.

I think of him
who taught us to hate sin
but to love the sinner,
who hated sin
because it makes us into murderers,
murderers with guns,
with words,
with seemingly insignificant actions
or with indifference,
whose love for people grew
because he knew
that we are all victims of sin
and that we cannot escape by ourselves.

I am thinking of him
who allowed himself to be crucified
because of those two attitudes
—hating sin
—loving the sinner
and in that way broke through the devilish circle.

And now I am ready
to shoulder my life
in the thought of you
Jesus.

3
Suddenly
I can see through those around me,
see the merciless imprisonment
from which they would like to escape
but don't know how.

4
How was your life?
What did you do as a teenager in Nazareth
a small city with many cliques
and with much gossip?
Who were your friends?
How did you get along with them?
What did your parents expect from you?
Could you live up to their expectations?

How was life with your disciples
who misunderstood you so often?
Did you not feel betrayed
long before Judas actually did it?
And did you think of giving up,
in Gethsemane or at other times?
How frustrated were you
when you said to your disciples:
I have many more things to say to you,
but you cannot bear them now.

How did you survive the jokes
of those around you?
Where and in what did you participate
and how did you know your limits?
How did the others look at you
when you did not join in?

How would you live my life?

5

I see that you have entrusted
all of life to me,
the full life
between heaven and hell,
between intoxicating joy
and deathlike sadness,
between communication and loneliness,
between clarification and silence.

And I do not want to betray you Jesus
by withdrawing from life
and I do not want to betray life
by fleeing from life to you
because you can only be found
in the middle of life
and in the suffering-in-life.

I will live
I want to live
where you lived also
and where you still live:
in the middle of sin,
vulnerability and suffering,
in the anguish of living,
in the thousand emotions of awareness,

in me.

To Give Myself

1
How do I do it: to give myself to you?
I have practiced this for years
and I still don't know whether I can do it.
But I want to learn
by waiting on you,
but even the waiting comes hard to me
because I don't know how to wait.

What should I do?
What should I not do?
How far am I allowed to think?
Where should I sacrifice my will?
Where do I end and where do you begin?

2
I am noticing that there is something
I have never considered to be part
of my devotion to you:
giving up trying to know!
I am acceptable in my attempts to please you.
I am acceptable in my lostness.
I am acceptable in my waiting.
I am acceptable in my doing and not-doing.
I am acceptable in my thinking
and I am acceptable in the giving up
of my intellectual abilities.

Jesus
I am realizing that to sacrifice myself
means to believe that you are on my side,
that you have decided to be for me
and that you have proven this
when you died
for me.

Now I can be liberated of my striving self
because I do not have to do right
to be loved by you.
The love between you and me
has been there since eternity
and it is not conditional upon anything.
I just have to hang on to that.

3
Your love starts to grow in me
at exactly the time when I become unsure
and when I think you have forgotten me.

You are closest
when I least suspect it.

Silent Blackmail

1

Why doesn't my joy convince him?
Why can't he believe as I do
  and be happy?
Why isn't he radiant with joy
  when he has so much reason to be joyful?
What's the matter with him?

He hangs his head.
He talks of difficulties.
He talks of troubling thoughts
  which he does not want to share
or he is completely silent,
  as if he did not trust me to understand
  what he is experiencing.

I don't know how I should approach him.

2

I am noticing
that deep down I believe
that joy always expresses itself
in a beaming face

and because that is not the case in his life
I have assumed that he is not joyous
and for that reason I have tried to draw him
  out of his sadness
  with my joy
and I did not even notice
  that he was not sad.

3

Today I reacted to him
as I always do
but while I was with him
I tried to see myself in his shoes.

I talked to him
but at the same time
I tried to listen to what I was saying
and I was surprised:

I noticed the lack of genuineness
   in my beaming face.
I noticed that my joy
   was trying to blackmail him.
I noticed that I tried to make him feel guilty
   for not being as radiant as I was.

I am actually working against him.
I am putting him down.
I am reproaching him
   for not being like me.

I try to convert him
   to a smiling face,
   to a dead mask,
   to falseness.
I have tried to turn off his thinking
   by never taking his difficulties seriously.

I never really understood his silence.

4

I know that his being different
   annoys me,
   makes me feel insecure
because he does not act like I think he should,
because I cannot manipulate him,
because he is unpredictable,
because with his silence
he puts in question what I do.

5

I am now learning
that friendliness
(my friendliness for example)
is not always friendliness.

That I can bring the other person more joy
   by holding back my joy
   and sharing in his sadness,

when I meet him
   where he is
instead of trying to get him
   where I want him to be.

New Way or Wrong Way?

1
How am I to understand
that the others
    who know me so well
think that I am on the wrong path
when I am just trying to express
my faith in a new way,
to live what I feel,
to live what I can stand up for,
to reflect in my life
    what is going on inside of me?

Because I can't stand it any longer,
to continue something
    just because I began it once
or not to do another thing
    because I have never done it,
or not to think certain thoughts
    because they might be dangerous.

In repeating what has been said before
and in living what has been lived before
my faith dies
because it does not renew itself
by putting itself on the line.

2

I notice what others have noticed before:
the person who clarifies
   or tries to clarify
what is what in his life,
who tries to rid himself of false images,
who abandons articles of faith
   because they have long lost their meaning for him,
who is not willing to back up
   that which he does not believe in anymore,

this person
will be looked at as being dangerous,
as the one who causes confusion,
   who rocks the boat,
as a person to be avoided.

3

What can I do?
I will have to continue on my way
even if I am misunderstood,
even if others appeal to my conscience
   in an attempt to get me off the wrong path.

My faith
must be *my* faith each day.

4

But with each step
I notice the danger
of only reacting,
of only doing one thing
   so that I won't have to do another
and that is not enough.

I need your help Jesus
because while cleaning house
I do not want to lose
something that I should keep.

Sharpen my senses
so that I will notice when I leave you
on my new path,
when I lose you
in the attempt to come closer to you.

Help me on my narrow path
that leads between two alternatives
which are death to me.

5

While I am trying to keep my balance
you sometimes surprise me with a clarity
the like of which I have never experienced before,
because now I am not only an imitator,
not only a role-player,
not only a yes-man,
not a person who tries to please others
   and loses himself in the process.

I am a child of God
on the road into a full freedom.

6

I will hold my feelings back
so that they can reach a greater depth
before breaking out and meeting you.

Then I know
that my feeling is not only affectation
    in order to convey a certain picture of myself
    to you.
Perhaps then I will be able to convince you
    without effort
    and certainly without blackmail.

I also want to remain open for you
and for your way of seeing the world,
for the many disguises of joy and sadness,
because much is not
what it seems at first.

Guilty Conscience

1
Jesus
I notice my faith changing.
I am becoming aware that I do some things
    only as a form of pious work for you,
and I become ashamed of myself.

Now I am wondering
why I am reading the Bible,
why I pray
    and what my aims in prayer are,
what my motives are
    when asking for your will,
and why I talk about you to others.

And in this critical attitude towards myself
I notice that you become more valuable to me
because I can meet you as I am.

You are so close to me
    although I do not talk about your nearness.
I notice your hand in my life
    although I do not constantly ask to know your will.
My thoughts often circle around you
    although I do not call on you directly.

Why then
do I often feel
as though I am not doing enough for you?
Why do I have a guilty conscience?
What do you expect from me?

2

I am seeing my life
through the eyes of my friends and acquaintances
instead of trying to see it
with the eyes of God.

And I know
that my friends find many faults with me
    because I do not follow a certain style,
    because I refuse to fit into my prepared space,
    and because I sometimes offend that
    which has been stamped "holy" for many years.

And even though I know that
and understand the motives behind the expectations,
I have a guilty conscience
from which I can not liberate myself fully.

I have to learn to distinguish
    between the claims of God
    and the claims of the people around me
because ultimately I can only do justice
to the expectations of the people
    if I do justice to the claims of God first.

3

Jesus
I don't even want to ask
what you expect of me.
I want to stand before you
in the faith that you are holding my life
    in your hand
and that my life in you
    is not dependent on correct actions
    on my part.
I do not have to prove to you
    that I love you
because you know so much better
    whether I really do.

I do not want to fool myself
and I do not want to pretend before you.
I do not want to appease you
    with good works
    as though you were some pagan deity.
I am your son
and I want to live like your son.

In this certainty I want to rest with you.
I am not afraid to make mistakes
because not even mistakes
can separate us.

4

Perhaps we must go into the world
out of silence,
in order only to *live* God
and so to speak more loudly
than all abused and misunderstood words can speak.
To stand silently before you
is perhaps the greatest praise we can bring you.

5

My life has to be in constant change
if it is to remain the same.
What I am able to say with conviction today
   I can perhaps not repeat tomorrow
   without lying.
What I am singing of you today
   may be empty tomorrow.
What I am praying today
   might already have no meaning tomorrow.
And what I have to hold back today
   may have to be said openly tomorrow.

Being a Christian Without a Name

1
Sometimes I don't even want to use
the word "Christian" anymore.
It will only be misunderstood
    to the point that it will mean nothing
    to most people,
or it will mean something
    which is not connected
    to following Christ.

Then I just want to be a person
in the vulnerability of being human,
a man like Christ,
whose truth lay in his existence,
who *was* the word
and therefore needed to make few words.

2
When he lived
there weren't any Christians yet.
There were only people who hated or loved him
and both attitudes
showed in their day-to-day life.

3
The title,
the name,
the membership,
all came *after* Jesus.
All arose from the necessity to order
to systematize and to identify.

But now those with the name,
with the membership pass,
and with an organization backing them up
can hide behind their description
and it becomes much easier to follow the man
after whom we are named.

4
There is a blessing on the group,
but only
for the person
who does not hide behind the group
in order not to have to become independent.

5
We must bear our name
as though we did not have one.
We must live
as if each day were our first and last.

As a fixed point in our lives
we must have a person,
not a dogma,

Christ.

Wanting to Suffer

1
Why does this always happen to me?
Why me? What did I do?
Why must everything go wrong
with my friends,
at work,
in the church?

Why can't my life
be uncomplicated too?

I am afraid.
I become uncertain.
I don't trust myself anymore,
and even God is not secure in my life.

It seems as if my attention
is drawn towards the negative things in life.
Everywhere I see failure,
   difficulties and suffering
and I don't seem to be able
   to leave all that behind.

How can I get away from such a view of the world?

2

I notice
that I don't want to suffer,
that I avoid suffering,
that I run away,
    while God is looking for people
    who are willing to suffer with him,
    who are willing to penetrate
    to the mystery of suffering,
    who are not afraid to be afraid,
    who want to follow Christ through Gethsemane
        to Golgotha.

Jesus is looking for people
who are willing to stand
    where others run away,
    where I ran away,
who are willing to face the suffering,
    which lies open like a frightening wound,
    showing the lostness of us all.

3

I will remain standing
in the face of suffering.

I will stop feeling sorry for myself
to be free for the suffering of others.

I will ready myself
to be led into the mystery of suffering,
which is the heart of the world.

About the Author

Ulrich Schaffer is the author of such highly successful books as *Love Reaches Out*, *A Growing Love*, and *For the Love of Children*. A noted photographer as well, Mr. Schaffer often incorporates his excellent color and black-and-white photographs with his writing.

Love Reaches Out was winner of the 1977 *Campus Life* Mark of Excellence Award in Poetry and Fiction. His book *Searching for You* was selected Outstanding Title in the 1979 National Religious Book Awards. *Baptist Standard* called his recent work, *Surprised by Light*, "an unforgettable avenue of spiritual teaching that is implanted in your heart, mind, and soul for all time to come."

Born in Germany in 1942, Ulrich Schaffer moved to Canada with his family in 1953. For a number of years he has taught modern European literature in translation at a college in the greater Vancouver area. He writes in both English and German, and spends a part of every year in Europe giving readings and meeting with his steadily increasing audiences there. Married, with two daughters, Mr. Schaffer makes his home near Vancouver, British Columbia, Canada.